THE **HUSTLER'S** HANDBOOK

THE

HUSTLER'S
H A N D B O O K
A GUIDE TO SUCCESS
IN YOUR NEW CAREER

JASON POOLE

NEW YORK

NASHVILLE   MELBOURNE

THE **HUSTLER'S** HANDBOOK
A GUIDE TO SUCCESS IN YOUR NEW CAREER

Published in New York, New York, by Morgan James Publishing. Morgan James and The Entrepreneurial Publisher are trademarks of Morgan James, LLC.
www.MorganJamesPublishing.com

The Morgan James Speakers Group can bring authors to your live event. For more information or to book an event visit The Morgan James Speakers Group at www.TheMorganJamesSpeakersGroup.com.

Shelfie

A **free** eBook edition is available with the purchase of this print book.

CLEARLY PRINT YOUR NAME ABOVE IN UPPER CASE

Instructions to claim your free eBook edition:
1. Download the Shelfie app for Android or iOS
2. Write your name in **UPPER CASE** above
3. Use the Shelfie app to submit a photo
4. Download your eBook to any device

ISBN 978-1-68350-167-1 paperback
ISBN 978-1-68350-168-8 eBook
ISBN 978-1-68350-169-5 hardcover
Library of Congress Control Number:
2016912176

Cover Design by:
John Weber

Interior Design by:
Bonnie Bushman
The Whole Caboodle Graphic Design

In an effort to support local communities, raise awareness and funds, Morgan James Publishing donates a percentage of all book sales for the life of each book to Habitat for Humanity Peninsula and Greater Williamsburg.

Get involved today! Visit
www.MorganJamesBuilds.com

TABLE OF CONTENTS

GOOD THINGS HAPPEN
TO THOSE WHO HUSTLE

Cincinnati, Ohio, July 14, 1970: the Major League Baseball All-Star exhibition game. Thanks to a Brooks Robinson two-run triple, the American League took a 4-1 lead into the bottom of the ninth. But after a Dick Dietz solo home run and three singles, the National League put up three runs and forced the game into extra innings. Three innings later, National League batters were facing Clyde Wright. With two outs, Pete Rose and Billy Grabarkewitz hit back-to-back singles to put runners on first and second bases. Jim Hickman singled to Amos Otis in center field. Otis fired the ball to catcher Ray Fosse as Pete Rose ran past third base, heading to home. Otis' throw was on target, and arrived as

Rose reached Fosse. Rose bowled over Fosse, forcing him to drop the ball—and scored to end the game.

Twenty-three year old Ray Fosse suffered a fractured and separated left shoulder when Pete Rose collided with him on the last play of the game. By his own admission, he never regained his swing, and he never returned to the level of play that he'd been at before the injury. In a 1999 *San Francisco Chronicle* interview, he demonstrated that he still could not lift his left arm, and he now suffers from arthritis as a result of the injury.

Pete was heavily criticized for the play at the plate. At that time the All-Star game was, at most, an exhibition game that was largely played at half speed. When ESPN interviewed him after the game, asking why he went so hard, he simply said, "I was trying to win the game."

Once I saw Pete Rose play that game, I learned more and more about him. He wasn't the biggest or fastest or strongest guy on the field, but he played to win, every second of every day. This was my first glimpse of *the hustle*. I understood then that hustling was free for the taking, and that playing to win all day every day could make up for many God-given talents.

To me, the word "hustle" means consistent, devoted, hard work, and Pete Rose was the definition of it. In 1963, he won Rookie of the Year, and he never looked back. Whether he was running over the catcher in that All-Star game or diving into third base head first, he showed that he was willing to do what it took to accomplish his goals. Even after suffering a few very big mistakes (and who doesn't?), he's still seen as the quintessential example of what a baseball player should be by fans and MLB players alike.

How I Got into Hustling

Before I go any further, I want to say this: "hustling" no longer connotes a bad thing. We're not talking about slinging rock and swindling. We are talking about doing *work*, as Big Black from MTV's *Rob and Big* would say.

Pete Rose's rise to success gave me a little faith in myself. Like him, I didn't do particularly well in high school. In fact, I remember feeling a little bad for my parents—they'd both set pretty high expectations for making good grades. It did not help that my mom was the valedictorian in High School and held a 4.0 GPA through college and Nursing school, all while raising two boys. Going downstairs to the remedial class every day was pretty embarrassing for me, especially knowing that my friends were upstairs sitting in AP English and living it up with all the hot girls.

As a kid, high school is what everyone judges your future success on. When you fail at school, people expect you to fail in life. Not being good in school conditioned me to think small, and it made me second-guess the person that I aspired to be and things I aspired to do.

Since figuring out the hustle, I've spent most of my adult life doing what I know I am good at: busting my ass. I hated feeling that aptitude would determine my ultimate altitude. Once I realized that I had a choice about whether I felt terrible about myself, I decided to choose to feel good about who I was. I started to make things happen. No wall was too big for me to climb. With help from *many* people that I admire and appreciate, I was able to pull out of the pity party I was having for myself. Once I figured out what

I needed, I could work—and once I figured out what I was good at, I could enjoy it.

One of the biggest setbacks that I have ever endured happened just as I was starting to feel okay about the direction that I was headed in—that bitch Hurricane Katrina. I had a great new job at Express Employment Professionals, and I'd just bought a house and a car—and it was all taken away in about six hours. Overnight, just like so many other people, I lost it all.

I spent the next fourteen months living a bunch of different places: in a tent, in the office where I worked (thanks Robert!), couch-surfing, and in a FEMA trailer. Just like that, I chose to feel sorry for myself again. I threw one of the biggest pity parties ever—even the Kardashians would have been impressed—and I did this knowing so many people were worse off than me.

It's hard to get back up after a blow like that, but if you can look up, you can get up. Once I quit with the pity party, I was able to keep going. I'd accomplished something before the disaster, and I wanted to get back there, and get better. Luckily, the job that I had just landed at Express Employment Professionals survived the storm and had a spot ready for me two weeks after Katrina. My mentor, Robert Myer, was in charge, and he provided tons of support. Slowly but surely, I started sneaking up the organizational ladder. If there was a job that nobody wanted to do, that was the one I volunteered for, no questions asked. You need help in an office four hours away? I'm there. You want me to get everybody coffee? Decaf or regular? You want me to take a pay deduction? I'll handle it. You say jump, I say how high. And then I jumped higher.

It didn't happen overnight—I've been working for Express Employment Professionals for over ten years. I hustled like hell for five years before I got a chance to own a franchise of my own. I was able to get a small loan for an already failing franchise, and I was able to grow it to a point that I could sell it and purchase the office I first started with in Gulfport, MS. Two years later I opened my second franchise, and then a year after that, a third—with plans for four more in the next four years. Out of 752 franchises worldwide, my oldest Express Employment Professionals franchise ranks in the top 1 percent. I think we can get better, too. As my franchises started to grow, so did my interest in other business opportunities such as start-ups, real estate, professional speaking, and business consulting.

I'm on track to retire young from the daily grind—age forty has been the goal since college. I know the Hustle never subsides; by "retire," I mean not being restrained to one company in one location every day. Retirement to me, is having the freedom to see an opportunity and take, help others on my team chase their dreams and help them find a way to reach them, help lift others up outside of The Express Organization. I've gone from Point A—feeling crappy about my life—to Point B—my own version of success—and I know that there are a million Points in front of me to keep me on the route to success.

In the meantime, I'm focused on helping the future hustlers get on track to reach their Point B as quickly as possible. The reason? I'm paying it forward. I have been lifted by others and been shown how to hustle. I've extinguished stinking thinking and vacated pity parties. I have been given brilliant opportunities and the tools to capitalize on them. It's my life-long obsession to build an empire that gives others the same opportunity I had: to help themselves reach their Point B, to achieve success.

The Hustling Dilemma

It's pretty simple: the only consistent trait between people who have sustained success is *Hard MF'n Work*. However, there are definitely a few common problems that most people—myself included—face in getting to their Point B while enduring the Hustle.

- **You're waiting for the right moment**. First of all, a career path can be overwhelming when you look at the big picture with a small mind. Most people feel that they have to know exactly what they want, how to do it, and when they will get it, and then they'll wait for the setting to be absolutely perfect. I do agree that good things come to those who wait, but those good things are usually the stuff left behind from those who hustle.
- **You don't have a clear goal.** You can't hit a target you don't have. Keep in mind that the path doesn't always have to be clear before you take the first step. If you don't know exactly what your target is, then borrow one from someone until you figure it out. Where is your Point B? What do you want out of life? Until you figure that out, you can't commit yourself to getting there. I knew I wanted to retire early so I could spend

time with my family and give them everything they need, so I'm doing what I have to do to make it happen.

- **Stinking Thinking.** "Don't have a 3.0 on your transcript? You might as well be a garbage man for the rest of your life." That's not true, but that's how most people feel and think. The person that you talk to more than anyone is yourself, so be careful what you say—you just might start to believe it. Don't let the weather predict your day.

- **Getting locked into the Cycle of Mediocrity.** My dad always told me that you are who you hang around. Hanging around people who have an average mindset and who readjust their means to compensate for their laziness is dangerous to success, and an absolute blockade to Point B. You have to be careful about who you ask for advice. Be sure that you don't take advice from people who are stupid, or people who are currently in the same situation as you are. Instead, listen to those who are where you aspire to be. I think that we all aspire to give our children and ourselves the greatest opportunities for success. We inherently want the best for ourselves and those we love. If you're happy being mediocre, then you can't have the best for your children; you won't be able to give them everything they deserve and need. You can always do more, for both you and your children.

- **Laziness.** It's the worst problem of all. It takes a lot to build habit, but if you're not committed to anything, then you will succeed at nothing. Another form of this is entitlement. For better or for worse, none of us just automatically deserve anything. We have to make it all happen ourselves. Our country gives us the right to pursue happiness, and the pursuit is something that many are not willing to do. Take advantage of what those who've come before us have earned for us.

There are many ways to hustle, but I have picked up a few tips along my way that have helped me get on the track for success. I'm not a billionaire, but I've taken nothing and made it something—with the help of a *lot* of people. I've got it down, and as long as you keep hustling all day, every day, that "something" will become *everything*.

It's my hope that by the time you finish this book, you'll find that something, or you'll identify your Point B and get to that everything. You'll be armed with an arsenal of tools that will help you, too, get engaged in the hustle and eventually get married to success. Each person is different, of course, so some things may not work for you, or may be difficult for you to implement, and that's okay. Use what you can to make it work, and keep going. This book isn't the be-all, end-all. You'll find other books, other things to help you—some of which I have listed at the end of this book. Explore what might help you, get off your ass, and make something happen—*today*. So here's to you, and here's to the Hustle.

Chapter One

H: HELP OTHERS GET WHAT THEY WANT

You can have everything in life that you want if you will just help other people get what they want.
—**Zig Ziglar**, Motivational speaker

fter a class during my very last semester at college, I was talking to my marketing professor, Dr. Billie Allen. She'd asked what I was going to do after graduation, so I was explaining my plan to work for one of the larger casinos in the area, or maybe in banking. She started fishing around in her purse for her phone as soon as I said the word "casino," and once she found her phone, she proceeded to make a call.

I just stood there, confused, while she had a ten-second conversation and then hung up. Then she dialed a second

1

number, had another ten-second conversation, and hung up again. Finally, she looked at me.

"Meet me in downtown Gulfport tomorrow morning at eight," she said. "We're going to meet with George Schlogal, and then we're going to meet with the HR folks at the Beau Rivage Casino." I stared at her. George Schlogal was the president and CEO of Hancock Bank, one of the largest banks in the Southeast, and he just so happened to be a personal friend of hers.

It amazes me that something as simple as a quick phone call can completely alter somebody's life. Even though neither company offered me a job, the two meetings changed my course of life for the better. I've had so many conversations with my mentors that appear to be insignificant, but have really shaped who I am today. Dr. Allen was the first business-savvy person to really see potential in me. Every remark she made, no matter how small, helped build me up into the man I am today. In high school, I was a jock, I was "stupid," and I was never really looked at as one of the good kids. Yet for some reason, this brilliant woman thought that I had something special. She started helping me find opportunities that I never would have found without her—and the more I took those opportunities and surrounded myself with educated people who had what I wanted, the more I learned about myself.

Dr. Allen's help pushed me toward success, and I began to see how simple it was to just extend a hand out to someone. Without realizing it, I developed a philosophy about helping people that has benefitted both them and me to this day.

Nothing of significance in the history of the entire world has *ever* been accomplished alone. The relationships that you earn today—and I say "earn"

> Nothing of significance in the history of the entire world has *ever* been accomplished alone.

because you have to earn people's trust, which is the foundation of any good relationship—will either open or close doors for you. I've been fortunate enough to live by my own philosophy of helping people that when I come across the right ones, they help me too. On the other hand, I know that I've pissed off a few people in my life, and it's held me back in certain situations.

Zig Ziglar is the person who put my philosophy into words: "You can have everything in life that you want if you will just help other people get what they want." Zig believed in abundance. He lived his life as a baker, not a taker. If he ran out of pieces of pie, he baked another one. When you live by the Law of Abundance, you help other people get their pieces of pie, too.

By contrast, when you live by a mindset of scarcity, you're doing your best to hold other people back in the hopes of preserving a piece of the pie for yourself. I don't think that most people do this consciously, but it happens. Even if they love you, people will tell you that you can't or shouldn't do something because they're incapable of it.

Once I put my focus on putting other people first, I

> Even if they love you, people will tell you that you can't or shouldn't do something because they're incapable of it.

started to feel a kind of relief that I've never felt before. This philosophy let me do what I felt was right without worrying about someone outshining me. I learned to pass the credit and take the blame. In turn, this earned me relationships with people that were willing to go to war with me.

Helping the Boss

Early in my career, when I was a young sales rep with Express Employment Professionals, I was full of energy and eager to do what I was told. I didn't focus on thinking—I focused on *doing*. I knew that I had zero experience selling, and I'd have to make up for it with hard work.

Though I never prospered in school, I prospered in people, and in reading them and taking care of them. I didn't have to be smart to know that I absolutely needed to do what the guy who was paying me told me to, and to do it well. That was the thought I put into it: you tell me what to do, I do it, you pay me for it.

There were a lot of people around me that also had no experience in selling, and it seemed like they were busy really thinking through *what* they were told to do, rather than just getting it done. That mindset isn't going to help you in the long run, though. When starting your new career, the best thing to do is focus on actually doing work. Don't talk about the work or think about the work; stick to the doing.

When I started running my own franchise, between the resentful folks and the less seasoned staff members, I spent more time explaining *why* someone should do their job than teaching them how to do it. It seemed like it was a hassle for someone to do something that wasn't word-for-word inside their job description. It was a paradigm that I wasn't used to. When I was a kid, my dad told me what to do, and I did it. He was my dad, and I was the kid, and I was supposed to do what he told me to, and he took care of me. That attitude carried over into my work. I did what the boss told me to because he was the boss, and he paid me. I didn't realize that other people hadn't been brought up this way. Eventually, I changed all job descriptions in my company to "Do what you are asked to do, and then do more."

The point is that this is the first—and relatively easy—step in helping other people get what they want: help your boss. There's a certain selfless generosity that comes with helping people, but this particular step is strategic. The very first person you should help is the person that pays you, and the easiest way to do *that* is make them look good.

In my case, it started with me doing what I was told. I didn't waste my boss's time with a lot of questions, especially in the beginning. When my boss told me that he needed me to be at one office that was five hours away and another that was two hours away every single week, I said yes. I did not follow up his request with questions like: Am I going to get reimbursed for gas? How far away is it? What's the state of the office? Can I get a raise since this isn't really in my job description? Instead, I asked what the address was and told him I'd call him at eight a.m. when I got to the first office.

As I learned more about the company, my boss stopped having to ask me to do things. I just saw where the needs were and took care of them. It was all about helping him accomplish his goals and making him look good to his own boss. Looking now from my current position as a business owner, I can tell which of my staff members have the team's best interests in mind, and which staff members are concerned only about themselves. I return the favor to those who help me out by keeping them high on my list of priorities. They're the people I spend time with so that I can understand what *they* want and help them get it. When it works right, it becomes a healthy, community-driven cycle. It doesn't matter if their Point B is different from yours (and it probably should be); helping others toward their Point B will help you toward your own.

> When you focus on helping people for the right reasons, it becomes a healthy, community-driven cycle.

The Next Level

Helping the person that pays you is an obvious choice, but what about the people who work beside you? How do you determine who to help and who to avoid?

The trick is to really pay attention to people. There are a lot of jackasses out there, and the biggest jackasses are sometimes the hardest to spot. They do such a good job of being fake that you have no idea what's underneath. They act like they're doing everything they can to help you, when really they have selfish ulterior motives; everything they do is a calculated game to wear you down and put the spotlight on themselves.

Andrew Carnegie once said, "As I get older, I stop listening to what people say and just look at what they do." This is great advice, and true leaders will use it. They'll support their own behavior, and they'll observe who doesn't. Hold people accountable to their actions, and help them do it.

> *As I get older, I stop listening to what people say and just look at what they do.*
> —Andrew Carnegie

When people are not loyal to the absent—meaning they jump at the chance to speak poorly about others—let them know that you're not interested in talking about people who can't defend themselves. When people speak poorly about the company, speak positively about it. When people complain about not being trained, ask them what training they've given themselves. When people criticize the boss, emphasize your boss's positive traits. Do all this, and then find the people who are genuine. Find the people that work their asses off and that are positive about the boss and the company and the team. Find the people that can impact your career, and help them get what they want. Hang around those that want the same things that you want, or that already have what you want.

My initial life goal as an adult was to become a millionaire. About three years ago, I thought that if I could help five other people become millionaires, then I could make myself one as well. To that end, I've kept an eye out for those in my company who are really driven, those who want to be helped, and I help them climb the ladder like I did. All five of them started at the bottom like I did, and are now well on their way to becoming millionaires. Helping them get what they want has helped me get what I want. Those five know that if they keep performing at the highest level, it will help me in what

I'm doing for my franchises, and so I'll keep helping them move toward success. Help breeds success, and again, it's just a big cycle.

What five people could you help? (Check yourself and make sure they're not actually Jackasses. If they are, take 'em off the list!) What would be a good first step to helping each of them?

Pull, Don't Push

When you think about helping people, you might think of pushing them into an opportunity. This works sometimes, but more often than not, it puts a negative pressure on people. People grow at their own pace, and you have to allow for that. I was fortunate enough to be pulled up by people who had already done what I wanted to accomplish. They stuck by me when my growth stalled or I regressed, and they knew when to back off and give me time for growth when I needed it.

Instead of pushing, let people see you out front. Lead by example. They'll want to follow in your footsteps.

Close to a battlefield nearly two hundred years ago, a man in civilian clothes rode upon a small group of exhausted, battle-weary soldiers digging an obviously important defensive position. The section leader, making no effort to help, was shouting orders and threatening punishment if the work was not completed within the hour.

"What are you doing?" asked the stranger on horseback from across the trench.

"I am in charge of leading these men. They do as I tell them. We must fortify this position; the orders came directly from the top!" said the section leader.

"So why aren't you helping them?" inquired the rider.

"I'm the ranking officer here. These are my men," the soldier shot back indignantly.

"So why don't you help them?" the rider asked again, seeming vexed.

"I just told you why, but help them yourself if you feel so strongly about it!" the section leader retorted.

To his great surprise, the stranger dismounted his horse, removed his jacket and jumped into the trench along with the other men and helped until the job was finished.

Before the stranger climbed out of the trench, he walked down the line to congratulate each of the men for their success and thanked them for their hard work. Afterward, he wiped his dirty hands on his saddle blanket, donned his jacket and approached the young section leader, saying, "You should notify higher command the next time your rank prevents you from supporting your men – and I will happily provide a more permanent solution."

As he began to mutter a snappy retort, the young man found himself standing face to face with the stranger. The section leader fell utterly silent and snapped to the position of attention to render a proper (albeit shaky) salute.

General George Washington had just helped to dig his fighting position while he stood idly by. Without another word,

Washington mounted his horse and rode away, leaving the young leader with a new outlook on leadership.

Helping the Right People

John Maxwell, whose work I very much admire, talks about several laws of leadership (which I find apply to most situations). One of the laws that stands out to me is called "the law of the inner circle." According to Maxwell, the five people you spend the most time with, your inner circle, ultimately determine what direction you're headed

> **John Maxwell's _Law of the Inner Circle_**
> _An individual's potential is determined by the success of those closest to him._

in. If you're hanging out with a bunch of street toughs and pill-poppers all the time, your intelligence level is likely to drop. Even the incomes in your inner circle will start to average out. To help yourself, make sure that you are at the bottom of your inner circle. It'll challenge you. It'll raise the bar.

Remember that you can't help people who don't want to be helped. If they don't care what you're saying or they're not interested in helping you, then you're spinning your wheels. Move on. If I promote someone in my company who is already comfortable and not interested in taking on more responsibility, that person is not likely to rise to the occasion. In the long run, that won't help the team at all. You take on risk for yourself when you help people. It's not a risk to be afraid of, but it means that you have to be deliberate in your choices.

Who is in your Inner Circle right now?

1.

2.

3.

4.

5.

Who might be in an ideal Inner Circle...and how can you incorporate them into your life right now?

1.

2.

3.

4.

5.

All of these thoughts are about getting you to your Point B, and none of the other lessons in this book will help you if you can't make this one happen. As you're helping people, though, bear in mind that you can't have an ego about it. These things are strategic, but you can't be one of the manipulative jackasses who do everything to make themselves look good. It's hard— the human brain isn't really wired to do anything other than take care of itself, but we're still social creatures. We still interact with others. If you can learn to sacrifice your ego, do it right, and do it all the time, you will move toward your Point B—and so will everyone else. Be intentional about it. Follow through and know that helping people is a mutual effort. You can help yourself by making others shine.

The Seven Axioms for Workplace Success

Since assuming a leadership role, I've noticed a trend among employees: Many people believe their professional destiny is in someone else's hands.

People seem to prefer to have their destiny controlled by another person, even if that belief entails there is nothing they can do to protect themselves from being on the wrong end of a cutback or stuck at the bottom of the organizational ladder.

Perhaps this belief comes from a lack of confidence that they can make it to the top on their own. Or maybe this paradigm is due to a long list of failures or missed opportunities for which someone else is supposedly to blame.

Leadership does have influence on your professional growth, but for the most part, the decision of who stays and who leaves the company is based upon the individual employee's perceived contribution.

Translation: the power to either stay, grow, or go is up to you.

In most situations, **the future of an employee's job security rests squarely on the shoulders of the *employee*, not the leader**.

Valuable employees have the greatest potential for remaining employed or for finding another job in tough economic times. Unfortunately, most employees never learn what it means to be a "valuable" member of the team. These concepts just aren't taught at school. You may get lucky and learn from a mentor, but most people either learn these principles the hard way—through experience—or never learn them at all.

Drawing upon some of the concepts I've touched upon in this chapter, as well as my experience as a leader and employee, I've put together a list of seven simple axioms any employee can follow to stay employed and get to the top.

1. You are a commodity. What you do as an employee only has value if someone is willing to pay for it. If you want people to value what you do, then you need to deliver on the "implied promises" that are inherent in your job description.

At work, it is implied that:

- You will do your job to the *company's* standards.
- You will be honest.
- You will be on time to work.
- You will never exhibit inappropriate or off-purpose behaviors or act contrary to the good of your employer.

If you are not delivering on these implied promises, then that could be your reason for feeling stagnant in your position, or your boss's reason for sending you packing.

The better you are at delivering on the implied promises, the greater your value will be as an employee. The greater your value is as an employee, the higher the odds are that you will always be employed. Fight against, or ignore, these implied promises and you jeopardize your job.

2. The value of your work is determined by others, not by you. As an employee, you cannot tell others how valuable you are. You cannot declare how hard you work. You cannot determine the worth of what you do based upon your own perceptions of worth. Your boss—and more particularly, your customers—determine the worth of what you do as an employee. Your book of business and the growth or demise of your clients tells the story.

Find out what others expect from you in the workplace. Focus on your "customers" and what they want. Ask your subordinates, peers, and superiors what their expectations are. Learn *their* definition of success so you can work toward it. Don't assume you know what it takes to succeed. Ask those who have already succeeded.

Just because someone is in a position of leadership does not mean that they have always been in a position of leadership. In our organization, a leader earned their position, so ask what they did to get there instead of wondering why you're not there. Solicit the input of others and then match your performance and behaviors to the feedback you receive. You will succeed when you deliver what *others* expect from you.

3. You get out of life what you give. Make sure you give your honest and best effort at work. Show more interest in meeting the needs of the business, rather than your own needs. When you do all that you can at work to achieve the company's objectives while suspending your personal agenda, you will likely find that your personal needs will also be met. When you watch out for others, they usually watch out for you. Give all you can at work. Never put yourself in a position where others can accuse you of not doing your best.

4. Be supportive of your boss. Do everything within your power and ability to make your boss a hero. Discern his or her needs and objectives. Do your part (and more) to meet those needs and achieve the boss' objectives. Be responsive to the directives and commands of your boss not only to his face, but to others on the team. Express appreciation and show your support whenever possible. Very seldom in the business world can one succeed without the support of one's boss. The more supportive you are of your boss, the more support you can expect in return, particularly during tough economic times. Remember, what your boss says about you has more bearing than what you say about you.

5. Be supportive of your teammates. Help out whenever possible. Chip in when work needs to be done. Never engage in gossip, back-biting, or criticism of the members of your work team. Talk positively about your colleagues. Offer encouragement and support to your coworkers at every opportunity. Recognize the accomplishments of others and praise them liberally. Be a team player in all of your actions, words and deeds. How you interact with others at work says a lot about your value to a company.

6. Be receptive to and a champion of change. Change is inevitable in every job. Work processes continually evolve. Good workers are always looking for ways to accomplish their work faster, cheaper, and more easily. Never become complacent in your work. Always look for opportunities to improve. When changes come, accept them eagerly and adapt to them quickly. Be an early adopter of change and help others to change as well.

7. Tolerate the idiosyncrasies of your organization. Every company has something strange about it. Usually there is some trivial (or significant) thing about the way a company operates that bothers the employees. Good employees are able to look past it; it is this tolerance that makes them especially good employees. Poor employees whine and let it affect their attitude; it is their bad attitude that makes them bad employees.

The more employees complain or fight against the idiosyncrasies of their organization, the less they become a part of it. Good employees seek to build up their organization, while bad employees tear it down. Do all you can to be a non-complaining, non-criticizing employee. Understand that some aspects of the company that seem idiosyncratic to you may be in place for a reason.

Live By The Axioms

These seven axioms should constitute "normal" behavior for all employees at all times. Clearly they are important during a downturn in business, but even during the good times, employees should model these principles, for in good times, high-value employees are most likely to get promotions and pay raises.

Remember, you control your destiny at work. Accept these axioms, or reject them; whatever choice you make, you will reap the rewards, or suffer the consequences.

To get "H" down pat, remember...

✓ Relationships will either open or close doors.

✓ Help the person that pays you.

✓ Don't overthink. Just do the job you're paid to do—and then do more.

✓ Jackasses are hard to see, so look at what people do instead of what they say.

✓ The Law of the Inner Circle can either raise or lower the bar.

Chapter Two

U: UNDER–PROMISE, OVER–DELIVER

Keep every promise you make, and only make promises you can keep.
—**Anthony Hitt**,CEO, Engels and Volkers North America

I never really understood the dangers of over-promising until a screw-up of my own — not in my professional life, but in my personal one, which can be more important. A few years ago, I was living with my beautiful then-girlfriend (now beautiful #1 wife) Courtney. Every single night, I had about a 2.5-hour commute home, and every night around five o'clock she'd call me to see when I was leaving. A couple hours later, she'd call to confirm when I thought I'd get in, and by then I was usually on the road. Every time she called to confirm, though, I over-promised. It wasn't ever a huge over-promise, really—if I was forty-five minutes away, I'd tell her I'd be home in thirty, or if I was five miles away from a certain exit, I'd tell her that I was already at the exit. I didn't want to look like I was taking my sweet time, and I didn't want her to feel bad. But every single night when I got home, there was always a sense of disappointment, because I never made it at the time I'd said I would.

Courtney never called me out, but at some point I realized the extent of her disappointment, and that even something as small as this was bad for our relationship. Now, I tell her I'll be home in forty minutes when I'll really probably be home in twenty. It means I'm not late every day in the way I used to be, and when I hit unexpected traffic I still make it on time. By under-promising, I've made it easy to do what I say I'll do.

Early on in his career, one of my mentors, Robert, told me his own story of how over-promising caused trouble in his professional life. He was loving his new job at a renowned insurance company. So far, he'd done really well with the "H" part of the Hustle—helping others get what they want. As a result, his boss had started giving him more and more responsibility.

Everything was going really well for Robert until one particular project came up. His boss, Mike, was supposed to be away on a business trip until the end of the week, and Robert figured he had all the time in the world to get to it.

Two days before Mike was due back from his trip, he gave Robert a call.

"How's the project coming?" Mike asked. "Are you finished yet?"

"Oh, definitely," Robert said, looking at the clearly unfinished project and thinking he still had plenty of time to finish it while the boss was away.

"Great!" said Mike. "I got back early and I'm just down the street. I'll be right over to take a look at it."

Of course, then Robert had to explain that he wasn't really finished and that he'd just said yes to look good. It didn't go over well.

Most people are familiar with the concept of "little white lies" in the context of work. They're lies to placate the boss; small yet important statements to make you seem like you're on top of things, even if you're minimally behind. But, as Robert learned, the little white lies can get you into a lot of trouble.

If people can't trust you for the small things, they definitely won't trust you when it comes to the bigger issues. Robert could've easily said that the project wasn't done yet and left it at that—the original deadline wasn't until the following week— and instead he screwed himself over. If he'd told the truth about the status of the project and finished it early, or even on time, he would have made an impression because he met or exceeded expectations.

The Space Between

The space between expectations and reality can give you an idea of how and why people do or do not trust you. That space can either represent disappointment or pleasure, depending which is on top. When we have expectations that are set high and then reality falls below it, that space represents disappointment. When reality is above the expectations, it creates pleasure.

Over-Promise, Under-Deliver

Expectations
Disappointment
Reality

You set your expectations either with words or past performance. You set reality with your current or future actions.

You set your expectations either with words or past performance. You set reality with your current or future actions.

> You set your expectations either with words or past performance. You set reality with your current or future actions.

Most of the time, we choose to set our own expectations high, hoping to impress the people around us. And yes, sometimes we meet those expectations, and even exceed them on occasion. Usually, though, we fall short of our expectations. This inevitability means that we're likely conditioned to think that most people aren't going to do what they say they'll do.

Under-Promise, Over-Deliver

Reality
Satisfaction
Expectations

Under-promising and over-delivering is not about underperforming and setting expectations low. It's about giving yourself the opportunity to ensure that you'll do what you say you will, and to condition the person or company that you are setting the expectations for to be amazed when it happens ahead of schedule. When setting expectation with clients and prospects, though, be sure not to set the bar too low. You should be performing at a high level, and you just need to set the bar to a level that you know you can meet and exceed.

There's a lot of debate online about whether this philosophy should be used. I'm not sure about everyone else, but this philosophy has helped me gain an edge on my competition and create raving fans.

Letting Yourself Get Ahead

When you under-promise, you automatically give yourself the chance to over-deliver. Let's say you get a deadline of January 1st to complete a project. Make your own deadline four days prior. It's all mental, and with a mindset that four days early is on time and on time is late, you can start to capture trust and knock the socks off of your boss. Why would they not be impressed when you continue to deliver quality work ahead of schedule?

To condition yourself to over-deliver when you get a project date from a superior or client, tell yourself the deadline is a couple days early, and put it in your calendar. When you know you need to be at work by 8:00, set your own standard to be there at 7:30. This is best illustrated by thinking about how much a field goal kicker over-delivers on an extra point. He doesn't kick the ball just enough to get it over the goal

> By under-promising, I've made it easy to do what I say I'll do.

post. He kicks the ball with enough might that even a deflection or wind or bird or plane won't keep the ball from passing over that goal post.

By under-promising, I've made it easy to do what I say I'll do.

A Little Heads Up Goes a Long Way

I work on under-promising with my team too. For example, if they're going to be late, they have to let me know way in advance. If you call right when the meeting starts at eight a.m. to say that you'll be late, it's obvious and it's annoying— it's already eight a.m. and you're not here, and you're not impressing anybody.

This rule has helped all of us maintain trust in each other in a big, big way. Everyone does the courtesy of letting people know in advance. Frankly, 75 percent of the time, they don't end up being late anyway, but even if they are, by giving fair warning, they've shown respect for the other people in the environment.

Everyone has an opportunity to either improve or hurt a relationship just by the commitments they make on a daily basis. Wanting to impress people is a natural human instinct, so think before you set your expectation and visualize that space between it and reality. Do you want the space to be filled with disappointment or pleasure? By making this simple change in your life, you'll improve your existing relationships, forge new ones, and open more doors for yourself—all of which will shoot you right toward your Point B.

Think before you set your expectations and visualize the space between it and reality. Do you want the space to be filled with disappointment or pleasure?

Like hustling, this is all free. It just takes enough effort and discipline to keep it going. According to Gary Keller, author of *The One Thing: The Surprisingly Simple Truth Behind Extraordinary Results,* you have to keep at that effort and discipline for sixty-six days to make something a habit. Once you make it a habit, it becomes easy—the process is engrained in you. You don't have to think about it as changing for a whole lifetime; you just need to work on it for sixty-six days and then it's part of you!

> Think before you set your expectations and visualize the space between it and reality. Do you want the space to be filled with disappointment or pleasure?

Apply this notion to under-promising. We all over-promise. Being aware that you do it is the first step to making it better. And again, like hustling, if you even deliver on 90 percent of the things you say you will, you've gotten further than most people. You've set yourself up for success, and all it takes is a little forethought.

What could you start to under-promise on, today? Write down exactly what it is and how you'll do it.

Is it as simple as setting the precedent for being on time to meetings? What about deadlines? Consider three options, list them here—and then commit to making them happen.

1.

2.

3.

Under-promising, first and foremost, is a habit. And just like habits are hard to break, habits are hard to make. Use this page to count some victories, big and small.

Victory #1:

Victory #2:

Victory #3:

Victory #4:

Victory #5:

Victory #6:

Victory #7:

Victory #8:

Remember that if and when you fail to under-promise, don't beat yourself up. Learn from it, and keep counting the wins. You'll keep winning.

Chapter Three

S: SACRIFICE

*Until you find something that you are willing to die for,
you are not fit to live.*

—Dr. Martin Luther King, Jr.

I work a lot, and I mean *a lot*. I also spend a lot of time with my family—*a lot*. Between all that, I don't have much "free" time. So many people shake their head at me and say, "I don't know how you do it!" To me, though, it's a given.

The word "sacrifice" gets a pretty bad rap. People hear it and automatically think something terrible is about to happen. For me, though, it's more about paying attention to what's important. I'm willing to sacrifice time at the bar with some buddies to hang out with my family. I look at all these pictures of my friends with families on Facebook, having the time of their lives out at the bar or out fishing with other friends, and it seems to me like they're the ones who are really making a bigger sacrifice. They're sacrificing time with their families and work for time with themselves.

> Sacrifice gets a pretty bad rap, but really, it's all about paying attention to what's important.

Sacrifice gets a pretty bad rap, but really, it's all about paying attention to what's important.

That's the thing. You have to be able to identify what's important to you in the long run, and then you have to commit to it. I'm okay with giving up golf, fishing, hunting, going out to the bar—because I'll be able to enjoy those things later. At this point in my life, I want to focus on being a great dad. That means that I'm going to give all the time in the world to my family, and that I'm going to do the best that I possibly can at my job, so I can give my family everything they need. When my kids are grown, I can go play golf. Right now, it's about putting together lasting memories so that they can become the best versions of themselves.

> If you have not painted a picture of what you want your life to look like, don't wait for it to appear, just start painting.

If you have not painted a picture of what you want your life to look like, don't wait for it to appear, just start painting.

If you're not really sure of the specific things you want in the long run, no sweat. Just get moving. Here's why—when you do eventually figure it all out, you'll already have a foundation to start with. You could spend all of your time and money right now screwing around and then have to start from scratch later on, or you could start now and be that much closer to your Point B, once you decide what it is. Every step of the Hustle is about setting yourself up for success. This is no exception.

What Will You Give?

So you've figured out what you want (or you haven't, which is fine too!). What are you willing to give to make it happen? The quote by Dr. Martin Luther King, Jr. at the beginning of the chapter is one of my favorites: "Until you find something that you are willing to die for, you are not fit to live." You have to want to succeed as badly as you want to breathe. When you want it that badly, it doesn't look like a sacrifice. It looks like a path. Dr. King indeed gave his life for what he wanted. Think about it. What do you want more than anything? What are you willing to give?

You have to want to succeed as badly as you want to breathe.

> You have to want to succeed as badly as you want to breathe.

Don't set anything as a goal if you're not going to commit to it. If you are not willing to do what it takes to lose the 100 pounds or make the million dollars in salary, don't talk about it. It won't happen because you don't want it badly enough to make whatever sacrifice is necessary. If you want to be fat, lazy, broke, or homebound, it's okay, but don't tell people you want to do something until you are willing to sacrifice what it takes. People won't be willing to help you if you're not willing to help yourself (see Chapter One!).

Wait for Pay Day

When it comes down to it, sacrifice is a pretty simple thing. If you sacrifice the right things at the right time you will eventually end up with the right things all the time. It can start early, and once you've built the habit, you can do more with it later. Can I sacrifice buying this candy now so that I can buy that CD later? Can I sacrifice a night at the club for a night of taking care of myself? Can I sacrifice buying that fancy convertible with money I don't really have right now so that I can invest in my future? Can I just sacrifice talking about myself so that I can listen to others? Sometimes you have to sacrifice short-term solutions for long-term opportunities. Get over the instant gratitude so that your hard work will pay off for you later.

Early on in my career, Robert used to tell me that I should be driving around looking for real estate on the weekends instead of making $40 cutting grass. At the time, I had bills to pay, and my salary at the time made that hard. Looking back, though, I can see that I would be way ahead of where I am now if I could've gotten myself out of that poor mindset. Investing time is just like investing money. Again, you just have to sacrifice short-term solutions for long-term opportunities. It's hard to understand or even support when you're really broke, but it pays off.

> You have to sacrifice short-term solutions for long-term opportunities.

You have to sacrifice short-term solutions for long-term opportunities.

At the time that I was focused on cutting grass, I was only making about $17,000 a year at Express Employment Professionals. I knew it wasn't great—I was mowing lawns like a teenager to supplement it—but at the time I thought that this was the only way to survive. All the same, when my friend showed me the letter offering him a promotion and boosting his salary to $52,000, I couldn't help but think that he was rich. He thought so, too.

It was hard for me to be a sales rep. I spent so much time out in the field that I got offered jobs all the time. There was one offer in particular that I struggled with a lot, because it really couldn't be beat. The guy was not just going to triple my salary, but he was going to give me a car, a phone, and a position of real power.

I thought about it for two weeks. Everyone I knew told me to take the job, and I didn't blame them. Ultimately, though, I turned it down. I felt like it was more important to stay on with Express Employment Professionals, since I'd already worked so hard to establish myself. I knew that in sticking with it, I could earn myself power, money, *and* security.

In the end, I did help the client find someone else for the job. Less than a year later, the guy was laid off without notice and immediately replaced. Every time I see the client's name now, I wonder how things would've turned out if I'd taken that job and ended up in the same position. Maybe I would have bounced back, but maybe not.

What I do know is that my decision to sacrifice the instant gratification for long-term success was the right one. People move from job to job for less than an extra dollar an hour, and most of the time, they end up in the same place that they started. They're not willing to be patient and let things improve over time. Careers—and goals in general—are like oak trees. They don't grow strong in a day. They grow with time and nourishment.

Remember to Sacrifice Your Ego

In Chapter One, I talked a little about sacrificing your ego. One of the things that I am reminded of on a daily basis is that it's not all about me. I have my kids to help me remember that! It's true of other people too, though. You don't exist just to protect yourself and your family. Remember, the cycle of helping others is a *cycle*, and it's one that creates opportunities all around. You can't help others with your own interest as the only goal. Helping others is all well and good, but if it doesn't come from a genuine place, it's not going to come back to you. If you're going to help others, you have to put them first. Remember to give credit to other people, too, where credit is due. Prioritize others…and they'll prioritize you.

> Remember, the cycle of helping others is a *cycle*, and it's one that creates opportunities all around.

Remember, the cycle of helping others is a *cycle*, and it's one that creates opportunities all around.

Quit Keeping Score

Rich Dad, Poor Dad by Robert Kiyosaki is a book that you'll find on my reading list. One of my favorite principles that I took away from it was "working for free." Having given it some thought, I now work for free a lot—meaning that I'm willing to do things for my companies and people without taking a salary for it. I do it because I understand that I'll be paid back in the future, or repaid in some way that isn't monetary.

Someone once did me a big favor, and I told him I'd buy him lunch to pay them back. I don't even remember the situation or who it was, but I'll never forget what he told me: "Don't bother. I don't keep score."

I didn't understand what he was saying at the time, but it's now become one of the biggest rules I live by. When you try to keep score with people, you're constantly thinking about what someone owes you instead of what you can do for someone else. Took the trash out for your neighbor? Then you expect them to do it for you next time. When we think that way, we get bogged down by the scoreboard. Doing things for other people and expecting nothing in return is the biggest sacrifice we can make, mostly because it requires us to have no ego and to delay recognition.

I've found that it always comes back to you. You forgot your wallet? No problem, I've got dinner, forget about it. This kind of behavior lets people off the hook for minor problems, and it builds trust. My boss never felt like he had to pay me for working excess hours early in my career, and I always knew it would come back to me. It has definitely come back to me. I helped him, it built trust between us, and in turn, he helped me get to my Point B.

To get "S" down pat, remember...

✓ Figure out what you want, and figure out what you're willing to give up to get it.

✓ Sometimes you'll have to give up short-term solutions to gain long-term opportunities. It's okay. Do it anyway.

✓ Remember "H"...and sacrifice to help others.

✓ No more keeping score..

THE BALANCE BETWEEN
WORK AND LIFE

Something that people often struggle with is the balance between their professional lives and their personal lives. One of the simplest ways to deal with this is to make sure your professional life is in alignment with your personal one. Go back to the idea of giving your kids the best life they could possibly have, for example. In order to do that, you have to excel at your job in a way that both makes you money and allows you to have time with your family.

If you need time to yourself, take it. One of the keys to managing all the aspects of life is taking care of yourself. If you need a day at home to recalibrate, take the day. Don't push yourself in a way that will be detrimental to both your career and your relationships.

Work will change, and sometimes, it will go away. At the end of the day, work is a choice, and it's your choice as to which type of work you want to do. Family, on the other hand, is singular, and it is forever.

You can't get time back with your family, but you can maximize it. I read a study recently saying that parents spend an average of only seven minutes a day talking to their children.[1] *A second article I read in the* Washington Post *stated that parents are now spending around ten hours a week with their children.*[2] *Whatever the number, it's clear that getting in that family time is difficult.*

It really can feel like walking a tightrope. When we're at work, we feel like we should be at home. When we're at home, though, we feel like we should be at work. The end result is that we never really end up being anywhere—we're never fully present in what we're doing.

Make time for the important things with your family. Even if you're short on time, just be in the moment when you're there. Quality is important. If you're at work, be at work. When you're at home, turn off the phone and the TV and be in the moment. Engage. Do your best to schedule work events around life events— and not the other way around.

---

1   http://www.thedadvibe.com/parents-spend-less-than-7-minutes-a-day-
       talking-to-kids/
2   https://www.washingtonpost.com/local/making-time-for-kids-study-
       says-quality-trumps-quantity/2015/03/28/10813192-d378-11e4-8fce-
       3941fc548f1c_story.html

Chapter Four

T: TAKE CHANCES

If you're offered a seat on a rocket ship, you don't ask what seat. You just get on.
—**Sheryl Sandberg**, Facebook Chief Operating Officer

W hat's the biggest chance you've taken lately? I can think of a million that anyone anywhere could face. Driving to work is taking a chance. Going to college is taking a chance, and so is choosing not to go. Walking down Bourbon Street during Mardi Gras is *definitely* taking a chance.

Basically, every decision you make is a chance. There's risk involved, whether you turn left or right, whether you walk down the aisle or get in the limo and drive away. When I say "chances" in terms of hustling, though, I mean the ones that are calculated to put us one step closer to our goals. How many opportunities do we let fly because of the fear of taking chances or fear of the unknown?

> How many opportunities do we let fly because of the fear of taking chances or fear of the unknown?

The answer is *too many*. All of us do it, and I'm far too familiar with the opportunities I've missed even when the door is wide open. Early on in my career at Express Employment Professionals, there was an area in the region that didn't have one of our offices. The territory was based out of Mobile, AL and was about fifteen minutes from my house. I was new to Express Employment Professionals, but I still knew that it was a growing company, and I knew for sure that one day I wanted to own my own franchise. My problem was that I could never get past the idea of "one day." I never did anything about making my dreams come true.

The option to purchase the territory in Mobile was the perfect opportunity, but I was afraid to take the chance. I told myself that it wasn't the right time. I told myself that I didn't have the money, or the experience, or, really, the guts to move forward. I was waiting for all of the lights to be green, and it never happened. It wasn't until later that I realized that ending up in a perfect environment with all of those green lights visible is a rare scenario.

This is a pretty sad story, because I chose to do nothing. I didn't take the risk, I ignored that scary thing, and the opportunity went to someone else. That territory was actually purchased a couple years later by Chris and Angela Ashcraft, who have since become great friends of mine. They've successfully grown the Mobile franchise to one of the biggest in the country. Chris and Angela were named Franchisees of the year in 2015, and they've recently opened another office in a neighboring territory. I'm so happy for them...and I can't help but look at their situation and know that it could've been me. Instead of jumping on it, I waited until the opportunity passed me by.

Fortunately, Chris called soon after to alert me that an office was about to hit the market for a rock bottom price, and all of a sudden I had the inside track to purchase my first franchise at a great price. I wasn't about to let this new opportunity pass me by, and I hustled to get that office. It paid off.

I recently told Chris about my apprehension in buying the Mobile territory, and he laughed and graciously thanked me for passing on it. Even though I did ultimately end up pulling the trigger and gaining the success that I'd wanted, that success could have been doubled just by taking a chance and walking into that unknown.

In 2012, my business had really started to flourish. One of my closest friends was working with me: Chad Purdy, aka the absolute King Kong of sales. Chad was killing it as the Sales Manager and bringing in business hand over fist. We were filling job orders as fast as possible and doing the absolute best we could with just the two of us, but we just couldn't keep up. We both knew that we were at our capacity and we needed to make a change, quick. At the time, my good friend Jared was living in Colorado. Jared was a very successful real estate agent, and he's one of the smartest and hard-working people I know. It seemed to me that he might be our missing piece.

I made a call to Jared after work one day and ran my plan by him. I didn't have to sugarcoat my words. We both knew that I had something special going on and he needed to be a part of it—a rocket ship with an open seat!—and I knew that we needed Jared's help to take us to the next level. Jared was immediately on board, and three months later, he, his wife, and their newborn son moved to their new house in Mississippi to join me and Chad in our quest to build an empire.

I tell this story for a couple of reasons. Think about that quote by Sheryl Sandberg at the beginning of the chapter. Jared recognized that he'd been offered a seat on a rocket ship, and he got on and brought his family with him. He trusted me when I told him we had something good in the works, and he took a chance on me—and he took a chance on himself, too. Jared has recently divorced and moved on to bigger and better people in his life. Even though the move may have caused this change in his personal life, it was a positive change and he is better because of it.

Confidence, Courage, and Chris Columbus

> *You can never cross the ocean until you have courage to lose sight of the shore.*
> **—Christopher Columbus**

I'm definitely not a fan of the morals of Christopher Columbus or the idea that he "discovered" America, but I

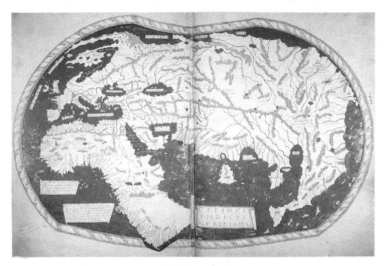

"Columbus, The 4 Voyages" by Laurence Bergreen

am a fan of the above quote, and of the chances he took to accomplish his goals. By the time Columbus set sail, most of the civilized world already knew that the world wasn't flat. What they didn't know was just how big the ocean was. There were a lot of myths and theories, but in 1492, GPS systems were pretty scarce.

Columbus was determined to find a faster sea route to Asia than the standard one of the time, which took seafarers all the way past the southern-most point of Africa and back up. No one was willing to take a chance on him, though, and he exhausted at least three possibilities of financial sponsorship before finding a solid investor. I can't help but think of the dedication it must have taken to keep trying after so many big rejections, and I admire his courage. He had the willingness, grit, and guts to look into the horizon with nothing in sight but the Atlantic, and then hop on a fifty-foot boat to try to cross new territory. Columbus must've been a hell of a salesman, too, because he somehow convinced eighty-seven other people to take the ride with him.

My feeling is that Columbus could pursue his dream so fearlessly because he had confidence in himself. He knew deep down that there had to be a better route to take, and so he went out to find it even when others didn't believe in him. I've learned to bet on myself every time, because if I don't, no one else will either. *You* have to take the chance, because no one will do it for you.

> *If you're not willing to risk the unusual, you'll have to settle for the ordinary.*
> —**Jim Rohn**, entrepreneur and speaker

Remember the Cycle of Mediocrity from Chapter One? Taking chances is the one way to break out of it. There's no way to hustle without taking risks. Columbus went off the map because the solution he'd been given, the current route to Asia, wasn't efficient enough. It was wasting time and energy and money. It was mediocre, and Columbus knew that something better was necessary—and possible.

If you're not willing to risk the unusual, you'll have to settle for the ordinary.
—Jim Rohn, entrepreneur and speaker

That's what taking a chance is: going off the map and charting new waters. When you take a chance and it doesn't work out, you're that much better than just sitting on the sidelines with your finger up your ass. You're doing work. You're hustling. If you fail, you still end up somewhere new, and you still learn something. If you win, you win, and you're that much closer to Point B. Timing won't always be right, your financial situation won't always be right, and the lights won't always be green. Take a chance anyway. The time is now.

Think of an upcoming challenge. What could happen if you take the risk? What will happen if you don't?

Chapter Five

L: LISTEN MORE THAN YOU TALK

One of the most sincere forms of respect is actually listening to what another has to say.
> —**Bryant H. McGill**, Founder,
> Goodwill Treaty of World Peace

A friend of mine is constantly talking about the difference between *listening* and *hearing*. *Hearing* is an action, but it's a passive one. If you're hearing something, sure, the words are going in one ear—but are they going out the other? *Listening* is 100% active, just like hustling itself. When you're listening, you're paying attention. There's no way to be an effective worker without paying attention to the people around you, and you definitely can't be a leader without paying attention to your team, your team's environment, and the environment in the world around you.

A big theme in hustling is that whole "do unto others as you would have them do unto you" idea—the Golden Rule. Apply it to listening. Do you want people to listen to you? Do you want them to really understand what you're saying and respond the right way? Then you'd better start doing the same with them.

It's not just about losing your ego and shutting your mouth. When you're paying attention, you're really connecting with others. Science has proved this correlation between achievement and the ability to care for and connect with others, but you can observe it in life, too.

I haven't done research. I've just lived. Below are some of my absolute favorite quotes that, to me, capture the entire premise of listening and listening well. What does listening mean to you? Check off your favorites—and then live by them.

1. Wisdom is the reward you get for a lifetime of listening when you'd have preferred to talk. —Doug Larson

2. If you make listening and observation your occupation, you will gain much more than you can by talk. —Robert Baden-Powell

3. Listening is a magnetic and strange thing, a creative force. The friends who listen to us are the ones we move toward. When we are listened to, it creates us, makes us unfold and expand. —Karl A. Menniger

4. Most of the successful people I've known are the ones who do more listening than talking. —Bernard Baruch

5. Listening is being able to be changed by the other person. —Alan Alda

6. Everything in writing begins with language. Language begins with listening. —Jeanette Winterson

7. There is as much wisdom in listening as there is in speaking—and that goes for all relationships, not just romantic ones. —Daniel Dae Kim

8. The most important thing in communication is hearing what isn't said. —Peter Drucker

9. When people talk, listen completely. —Ernest Hemingway

10. Friends are those rare people who ask how we are, and then wait to hear the answer. —Ed Cunningham

11. The art of conversation lies in listening. —Malcom Forbes

12. You cannot truly listen to anyone and do anything else at the same time. —M. Scott Peck

13. We have two ears and one tongue so that we would listen more and talk less. —Diogenes

THE LISTENING WORKBOOK

In theory, listening is easy—but it's really a learned skill that requires a certain discipline. There are a few steps you can take to becoming a better listener, and there are entire books and seminars about it. Here's a quick rundown of what I've learned from those books and seminars, condensed into a few pages.

Step One: Identify Your Barriers

There are a lot of barriers that get in the way of listening—they're just like earplugs. Unfortunately, they're easy to overlook. Some of them you probably do without even realizing it, so this is a good time to practice self-awareness and listen to *yourself*, too. The four most prevalent are: assuming that you already know what others know; feeling that you don't need to know what others know; not caring about what others know; and worst of all, not wanting to know what others know, because it means

Hannibal Lecter of *Silence of the Lambs* had a great piece of advice that he offered to FBI Agent Clarice Starling (smart is smart, even if you're a serial killer): "Don't assume. Assuming makes an ASS out of U and ME." He wasn't the only one who said this—it's a modern proverb that even Oscar Wilde has used. The point is, assumption, all too often, leads to misunderstandings and a complete lack of real communication. When you make assumptions in conversation, people are usually thinking to themselves, "I wish this guy would just shut up so I can tell him what I know." Chances are, you have no idea.

you're actively avoiding the communication. When you're having a conversation, check yourself. Are you putting up any of these barriers?.

Step Two: Learn How to Listen

The word "listen" contains the same letters as the word "silent."

—Alfred Brendel,
concert pianist

So where do you start? By now, you have a good idea of some of the things that inhibit listening, but avoiding them isn't the whole picture. I don't just want to be successful—I want to be a good boss. In order to do that, I have to keep amping up my listening skills. When I first realized that I needed to improve them, I started with **the Gap of Silence challenge**.

The challenge: when you're in conversation with someone, all you have to do is leave two seconds of silence before you speak. Simple, right? Except this was harder than I ever could've imagined. I tried several times and failed miserably at first, but after about ten attempts it started to get easier. Eventually, I got to the point where I was able to get through entire conversations by just leaving that two-second window open.

The need to break a silence is so common, and it often comes from avoiding uncertainty. What are they going to say next? What are they thinking? What do you hope they won't say? And what response will they have to what you've said that you might not like?

The thing is that you'll receive so much more information by leaving a gap of silence than you would if you leapt right into responding. Chances are, the person will keep talking. The challenge helped me to understand that frankly, people have a lot to say. If you don't keep your mouth shut, you'll miss a lot of it. You'll respond without knowing the whole story or offer unwarranted advice, and your conversation won't serve the purpose that it needs to. I know now that when I'm not focused on listening, conversations tend to jump from one subject to the other, and a lot of times I walk away from them feeling like nothing was accomplished at all.

People like to feel important, and if you're not listening, that feeling of importance starts to fade away. I know this because I like to feel important, too. And who doesn't? Not being listened to is frustrating. This is a great place to institute that good ol' Golden Rule: Treat others as you want to be treated.

Most people do not listen with the intent to understand.
Most people listen with the intent to reply.
—**Stephen R. Covey**, author,
The Seven Habits of Highly Effective People

When first working on my listening skills, I assumed that conversations would last much longer. That assumption just made an ass out of me. The better I became at listening, the shorter the conversations were. I found that by letting other people fully get their stories out instead of cutting them off, I was able to either answer the question, give advice, or direct them to the right place in half the time.

Most people do not listen with the intent to understand. Most people listen with the intent to reply.
—Stephen R. Covey, author, *The Seven Habits of Highly Effective People*

Step Three: Learn How to Talk

Once you've learned to listen, you can finally learn to communicate. The two aren't unrelated, but the things you say are just as important to connecting as the things you listen to.

Talk *to* people as opposed to above them. Let go of your ego; you're not better than the people you're interacting with, and you don't need to prove to them (or to yourself) that you are.

Get to the point. You don't need to add frills to what you're saying. There are benefits to being diplomatic, but if you dance around what you really want or need to say, the chances of being misunderstood are high. Get to the point, say it simply, and say less. Your real point will come across clearly. Say what you mean, and mean what you say.

Taking Communication to the Next Level

By listening and speaking intentionally, you're taking huge steps toward communicating the right way. Remember, though, that connection—that higher level—is the best way to work with people. What drew me to John Maxwell's book was his thought that if you really want to succeed, true connection with people is key. While it may seem like some folks are just born with this skill, the fact is anyone can learn how to make every communication an opportunity for a powerful connection. In *Everyone Communicates, Few Connect*, he shares the Five Principles and Five Practices that can take your listening to the connecting level:

1. Finding Common Ground
2. Keeping Your Communication Simple
3. Capturing People's Interest
4. Inspiring People
5. Staying Authentic in all Your Relationships

The ability to connect is a major determining factor in reaching your full potential and reaching your Point B. It's no big secret! Connecting is a skill you can learn and apply in your personal, professional, and family relationships. Even if you're dealing with someone who complains incessantly, just try it. You might figure out the deeper reason for their complaints.

Connecting isn't a thing you just decide to do and then get it done. There are actually a few practices that will make you better at it. They're practices in empathy, which we all know is one of the few things that makes us human.

The first one is *action*. Most of us know it as body language, which allows you to connect visually with others. To connect through action, keep three things in mind:

- **Use your facial expressions**, because these visual cues communicate what you're thinking more than you might imagine
- **Move with purpose**, which demonstrates strength in a way that makes people want to confide in you
- **Maintain an open posture**, which will make people feel as though you're willing to listen to what they have to say

The second practice is *thought*, which will help you connect intellectually with people. The knowledge that you share should be experiential. Experience is the best teacher, and it provides a certain validity to what you're saying. You're not telling people what you'd hypothetically do, you're telling people what you have done that either helped you to succeed or taught you something. Experience, hands down, is a great persuader.

The last practice is to connect *emotionally*. It's the heart of the empathy theme. People may hear your words, but they feel your attitude. Make sure that you check your attitude in preparation for the listening you're about to do. People can sense your agreement or disagreement, and if they think it's negative, they'll hold back. If you think the person is a loser, that thought will reveal itself whether you want it to or not.

The easiest way to listen is just to start doing it, and to keep doing it. None of these things are practices that you can do once and then suddenly be a better listener. If you keep doing them and doing them all, you'll keep getting better. Remember that there's no limit to how good you can possibly be. Listening's a skill. Practice and you'll get better.

I can't stress, though, how important listening is. If you don't learn to listen, you can't do the very first thing on the hustle list: helping people get what they want.

To get "L" down pat, remember...

✓ Don't just hear, and don't just communicate. Listen, and connect.

✓ Practice the Gap of Silence Challenge.

✓ Allow people the opportunity to open up, which can be achieved by the Gap of Silence Challenge.

✓ Talk *to* people rather than *above* them.

✓ Respond from a place of experience.

SELF-AWARENESS

One of the tricks to listening—and success in general—is to be very self-aware. The aforementioned barriers to listening will be impossible to curb if you don't take a look at yourself. It's not just about how much you talk, either. What do you need out of a conversation?

Self-awareness generally will make you a better hustler. Until you're able to look to some extent at yourself and know your personality, habits, strengths, and weaknesses, you'll have a wall between you and success. When you know your abilities, you can work harder to improve the ones you're already good at and step up your game with the ones you're not so great at. Do you over-promise time and again? Make it a point to practice under-promising on even the tiniest things so that you can build a habit that will help you in the future. Are you already a good listener? Great! Find ways to get better at it.

Being self-aware is an ongoing process, and it's one that, if you keep up with it, will guide you on the way to hustling. Keep up the habit, and your connections with people will improve, as will your performance in life.

Chapter Six

E: EXPECT THE BEST OF PEOPLE

High achievement always takes place in the framework of high expectation.
　　　　—Charles F. Kettering, engineer

I wouldn't be able to do the best I can at everything if important people in my life didn't expect the best of me. I don't know if there's a mathematical correlation between your success rate and the amount of people who expect the best out of you. I do know, though, that if the people around you expect the worst of you, you'll probably end up in jail.

We as humans either rise or fall, depending on others' expectations. There's actually a concept in psychology called the Pygmalion Effect, where, if the expectations are higher, people

> If the expectations are higher, people will rise to meet them. On the other hand, people won't perform as well if the expectations are low.

will rise to meet them. On the other hand, there's the Golem Effect, where people won't perform as well if the expectations are low.

When I think of this principle, I always think about the coaches in my life. Coaches constantly expect more and more from us, pushing us past the point where we'd normally give up. I know how to work out and how to eat healthy, but without a coach I cheat on myself. When I have my trainer standing over me telling me to do five more reps, though, I'll do five more. When I know he'll ask me what I ate today at our session tomorrow, I'll eat what I'm supposed to eat. I do it because he expects me to, and I'm better for it. I'm faster, stronger, and healthier because he expects me to hustle.

I had three really great coaches in my life: a mother who never let me give up on my dreams; a father who showed me that building relationships with other people would always come back to me later in life; and a brother who taught me how to get up after an ass whooping. I know that I'll do better and be happier when they expect the best of me, so when I expect the best of other people, it helps them step up their game. In a way, this step of the hustle is connected to H: help others get what they want. When you expect the best of people, you're not just helping them get what they want; you're enabling them to get what they want by doing the best they can. It's harder to expect the best out of people than you'd think. We've all been let down so many times in life that really, how could we not feel jaded? That cynicism affects everyone, and it becomes a cycle. When people let us down, we expect the worst. When we expect the worst, we *get* the worst. So it's up to us hustlers to change the direction of that cycle.

My Mother, Karen expects the best of everyone, and not just family members, either. She's able to see everyone at their full potential. Frankly, it's a God-given talent that she has; not everyone has that kind of insight and that kind of heart. Something she's always said that stuck with me is that there are two stories. There's the story that you tell yourself, and there's the real story. When you expect the best from other people, you're telling the best story possible.

There are two stories. There is the story that gives the benefit of doubt and there is the story that paints the picture in the worst possible scenario. It is funny how anytime we are involved in a story we always give ourselves the benefit of the doubt, but very rarely do we give that same benefit to others.

> There are two stories. There's the story that you tell yourself, and there's the real story. When you expect the best from other people, you're telling the best story possible, until you know the real story.

I am guilty myself of seeing someone disciplining their child in the grocery store with strong words or a swift swat to the rump, and saying to myself, "What a horrible parent! If they would raise their children right they would not have to do that." Then, at the same time, I raise my voice at my own child for pouring a box of fruit loops on the ground. The difference is that mine seems to be justified, and it is much easier to judge others.

Steven Covey tells a story in *The Seven Habits of Highly Effective People,* when talking about seeking first to understand, of a time when he was on the subway and there was a man sitting silently while his three kids caused a ruckus. The children were yelling and crying, all while the man sat and did nothing. Steven writes that he thought to himself, "What kind of parent lets their kids act this way in private, much less on the subway?" After several more minutes of chaos, Steven approached the dazed man and said, "Can you do something about your children?"

The dazed man slowly looked up at Steven and said, "I guess I should. I guess I just did not notice. You see, we just left the hospital where we have been for the last two weeks. We lost her. I lost my wife, and they lost their mother, and I guess now we are all just lost".

When we understand the real story a shift in paradigm happens. So until we understand the real story, try to tell yourself the best story possible.

I've tried to take my mother's philosophy and implement it in my life. When I meet someone that seems like they could be a future leader, I treat them as though they're already that leader. By identifying what people aspire to be and then treating them like they're already there, you can give them a vision of what it would be like to get to that Point B. Everyone wants to feel important, and this, like listening, is a big way to do it. You have to tell yourself the story of what they are yet to become, and not look at them as what they are or have been.

Expect the best of yourself, too. Keep the people who think you can't do something out of your life, because after you hear that negativity a lot, you might just start to believe it. On the other end, if you want to be something you're not, do it. Start telling yourself you already are, and act like it. My mentor always told me to dress for the position you want to hold, not for the position you are in. Don't wait until you become a sales manager to start acting like one. Start today. You have to play the part before you get the part.

Use the space below to identify three people who have expected the best of you. Who are they? How did it change your life?

1.

2.

3.

Chapter Seven

EVERY DAY I'M HUSTLIN'

n my younger days, I was involved in Mixed Martial Arts. At first, it was something fun to do to get in shape. After training a lot, though, I started to get pretty good, to the point where I thought I could step into the cage as a professional fighter.

When I told my trainer I wanted to go for it, though, I didn't know that I was in for a pretty rude awakening. "Jason," he said frankly, "you're a sissy. You come in here at your convenience, hit the bags, roll around for an hour, and then leave. You're not a real fighter. It's dangerous to just walk into a cage with an opponent who's been training to whoop your ass for six months. Until you're ready to live and breathe fighting, I can't let you do it. Fighting is as pure of a sport as you can find, and in order to compete at a level where people will pay you for it, you have to commit. You have to go all day, every day, with no exceptions. Walking in the cage, just like life, ain't no dress rehearsal. This is the real deal shit, where people can and will get hurt."

He was right. I was not ready then, but I was ready to make a commitment. So I took the plunge. I made that commitment to go all day, every day for one full year.

Then I got my ass kicked.

My first fight lasted fifty-three seconds. The guy literally choked me to sleep. I woke up understanding why my trainer had pushed me to fully dedicate myself to what I was doing.

Then I got my ass kicked again. The second fight lasted longer (ten seconds longer), but I walked out knowing that getting punched in the face for money was not for me. If I could take being a husband, father, and top-notch businessman as seriously as I had to take fighting, though, I could be exceptional.

> Life ain't no dress rehearsal.

Life ain't no dress rehearsal.

So that's what I did. My mindset shifted to one of, "Life ain't no dress rehearsal." I moved up from being a talking representative to a serious sales professional, and got hustling. The training was over. It was time to pour everything I had into getting to the top.

If you make a sacrifice that you're proud of, great. You're allowed to pat yourself on the back and celebrate that victory.

Then you have to keep going, because if you stop, you'll lose sight of the endgame.

On the other hand, if you fail terribly at something, you don't get to stop either. What is required of a true hustler is to keep going even when you fail. You can call for help, and someone who supports you will be there to back you up. And when you get up, learn from the experience and do it better next time. Enjoy your failures, you earned them.

These last few pages are designed to help you get the ball rolling and keep it rolling. You'll find exercises similar to the ones you've already done, and even a reading list to use to keep expanding your knowledge base on all things you. You'll be able to use all of it to keep your eyes on—and get to—the prize.

We've talked this whole time about getting to your Point B, and tools to help you get there. In short, this is not rocket science, and you don't have to be a scholar to make it in this world. What you do have to be is a Hustler. You have to have the ability to put others first, set aside your ego, work through tough times, be thoughtful, be honest, and give people the benefit of the doubt as you would give yourself. This is not complicated stuff, but this is the stuff that winners are made of.

These practices can't just happen every now and then. This has to be a consistent action that becomes part of you. Be patient and give this change time to show you results. Life is no dress rehearsal, so let's go to work.

Do the Work

Now that you have a few tools to work with, forget it all for just a second. There are some questions here designed to help you get to the root of you. Take a minute and answer them—and then come back and see if you can't start to apply the rules of the Hustle to each one.

You'll notice that there's a full page to address each question. You don't have to fill it up just yet. Here's what you do: date the answers that you leave today. Then, come back later—in a month? Six months from now? In a year? —and answer the questions again. Date those too. Keep coming back to it. The hustle never stops, and nor should you.

Question #1

If you could live someone else's life at your Point B, who would it be? Why?

Question #2

Based on your answer to question #1, what are you going to have to change to get there? If you don't know specifics, no sweat—what's one small change you can make today to help you get to your Point B? What is it that you'd like to accomplish, and by when?

Question #3

What helped you determine the answer to question #2? What needs would you fulfill by getting to that Point B?

Question #4

What actions, big or small, are you going to take *tomorrow* to get you rolling toward Point B?

Question #5

What actions, big or small, are you going to take *next week* to keep rolling toward Point B?

Question #6

What actions, big or small, are you going to take *next month* to keep rolling toward Point B?

Question #7

What's something great that you've accomplished? What did you do to make it happen?

Question #8

How can you take the success from #7 and apply it to getting to your Point B? What one thing did you learn from that experience that will carry over to all other successes in your life?

COUNT. THOSE. VICTORIES.

Every victory, no matter how small, is a step toward your Point B. You've already seen the page at the end of Chapter Two that helps you count your under-promising victories. Keep in mind that all of these tips to help you hustle are habits. You can't help a random person once, expect it to make a huge difference in your life, and then never help someone again.

Use these next few pages to count your victories in all of the hustling categories, and circle which category they fall into (keep in mind that they can, and often will, fall into multiple categories!). Having them written down in front of you isn't just decoration for your walls—it's an indication for yourself that you're doing the right things, and a reminder to keep doing them! When you run out of pages here, keep doing it somewhere else. Give yourself that opportunity to win.

VICTORY

It's a H U S T L E

VICTORY

It's a H U S T L E

VICTORY

It's a H U S T L E

VICTORY

It's a H U S T L E

VICTORY

It's a H U S T L E

VICTORY

It's a H U S T L E

VICTORY

It's a H U S T L E

VICTORY

It's a H U S T L E

VICTORY

It's a H U S T L E

VICTORY

It's a H U S T L E

VICTORY

It's a H U S T L E

VICTORY

It's a H U S T L E

VICTORY

It's a H U S T L E

VICTORY

It's a H U S T L E

VICTORY

It's a H U S T L E

VICTORY

It's a H U S T L E

VICTORY

It's a   H   U   S   T   L   E

VICTORY

It's a   H   U   S   T   L   E

VICTORY

It's a   H   U   S   T   L   E

VICTORY

It's a   H   U   S   T   L   E

VICTORY

It's a H U S T L E

VICTORY

It's a H U S T L E

VICTORY

It's a H U S T L E

VICTORY

It's a H U S T L E

VICTORY

It's a **H** **U** **S** **T** **L** **E**

VICTORY

It's a **H** **U** **S** **T** **L** **E**

VICTORY

It's a **H** **U** **S** **T** **L** **E**

VICTORY

It's a **H** **U** **S** **T** **L** **E**

JASON'S RECOMMENDED READING

I'm not going to bore you with a lecture on how important it is to read and to keep educating yourself. What I will say is that by reading books, you first open yourself to mentors that you would not normally have access to, and second, once you hear or read something, you can never think the same way about it again. Reading takes you to a place you can't get to alone.

You know already that you need to do the work. So here's a jumping-off point. Find some time each day to read. You probably already spend a good amount of time in your car, too, so why not capitalize on it? The following list will provide you with a little over a year's worth of material. After you complete it, it's up to you to keep it going. You'll notice that most of these are geared toward an entrepreneurial perspective. *They are still for you.* The mindset that it takes to succeed in the business world is the mindset that it takes to succeed, period. Apply what you learn to everything.

JANUARY (Month 1)
READ   212 Degrees by Sam Parker

            Sales Tough by Sam Parker

No listening this month!

FEBRUARY (Month 2)
READ   QBQ by John Miller

            Seeing the Big Picture by Kevin Cope

LISTEN   Success and the Self-Image by Zig Ziglar

            See You At the Top by Zig Ziglar

MARCH (Month 3)
READ   Smile and Move by Sam Parker

            Rich Dad, Poor Dad by Robert Kiyosaki

LISTEN   How to Get What You Want by Zig Ziglar

            Secrets of Closing the Sale by Zig Ziglar

APRIL (Month 4)
READ   Fish by Stephen Lundin

            The One Thing: The Surprisingly Simple Truth Behind Extraordinary Results by Gary Keller

LISTEN   Leadership Mastery by Dale Carnegie

MAY (Month 5)
READ   Lead Simply by Sam Parker

LISTEN   5 Levels of Leadership by John C. Maxwell

            21 Laws of Leadership by John C. Maxwell

JUNE (Month 6)

READ   Who Moved My Cheese? By Spencer Johnson
            Do the Work by Steven Pressfield

LISTEN   101 Relationships by John C. Maxwell

JULY (Month 7)

READ   One-Minute Manager by Ken Blanchard

LISTEN   101 Attitude by John C. Maxwell
            15 Invaluable Laws of Growth by John C. Maxwell

AUGUST (Month 8)

READ   360 Degree Leader by John C. Maxwell

LISTEN   SEAL: 31 Days Training With the Toughest Man
            on the Planet by Jesse Itzler

SEPTEMBER (Month 9)

READ   The Seven Habits of Highly Effective People by
            Stephen R. Covey
            The Art of the Deal by Donald Trump

LISTEN   101 Mentoring by John C. Maxwell

OCTOBER (Month 10)

READ   Cross the Line by Sam Parker
            The Complete Lean Enterprise by Beau Keyte and
            Drew Locher

LISTEN   101 Success by John C. Maxwell
            Everyone Communicates, Few Connect by John
            C. Maxwell

NOVEMBER (Month 11)

READ It's a Jungle in There by Steven Schussler

LISTEN Contagious by John Berger

The Ultimate Sales Machine by Chet Holmes

DECEMBER (Month 12)

READ Primal Leadership by Daniel J. Goleman

LISTEN The Advantage by Patrick Lencioni

The Tipping Point by Malcolm Gladwell

JANUARY (Month 13)

READ The Secret by Ken Blanchard

LISTEN Developing the Leader Within You by John C. Maxwell

How Successful People Lead by John C. Maxwell

ACKNOWLEDGMENTS

To my beautiful wife Courtney. I could not do what I love, without you. You have given me the freedom to take chances and follow my career dreams without question. You have always been by my side, never complained, and always had my back. You are the true recognition of my souls counterpart. Audrey and Halle, thank you for helping me understand that life is not about me. You both have helped drive me to be a better person and put family before all. I want to thank my mother, Karen, for teaching me to be kind, honest and to never give up on people. And to my dad, Dale, for showing me the hustle. You helped me understand that the relationships today will help or hinder you in the future. You helped me learn how to turn nothing into something. To my brother Shannon, for never cutting me any slack, for all of the ass whoopings, and teaching me that life is not set up for sissies to succeed. To Chad, for making me want to get better every day and riding this thing out with me, even through the dark days. To Jared, for taking that seat on the rocket ship, I hope you feel like you made the right decision. To my team at Express for making me look like I know what I am doing. My editor for making my words and thoughts something that could be deciphered by a normal human being, and lastly, my publisher.

A free eBook edition is available with the purchase of this book.

To claim your free eBook edition:
1. Download the Shelfie app.
2. Write your name in upper case in the box.
3. Use the Shelfie app to submit a photo.
4. Download your eBook to any device.

Shelfie

A free eBook edition is available
with the purchase of this print book.

CLEARLY PRINT YOUR NAME ABOVE IN UPPER CASE

Instructions to claim your free eBook edition:
1. Download the Shelfie app for Android or iOS
2. Write your name in **UPPER CASE** above
3. Use the Shelfie app to submit a photo
4. Download your eBook to any device

Print & Digital Together Forever.

Snap a photo

Free eBook

Read anywhere

The Morgan James
Speakers Group

Morgan James makes all of our titles available
through the Library for All Charity Organizations.

www.LibraryForAll.org